BUDDHISM

A BEGINNER'S GUIDE

How to Find Inner Peace by Incorporating
Buddhism Into Your Life

M.E. Dahkid

ISBN-10: 1502719991
ISBN-13: 978-1502719997

DEDICATION

In Buddhism, the focus is not a god or deity but a way of life to find inner peace and avoid suffering brought about by worldly pleasures.

CONTENTS

Introduction   i

1   Getting to Know Buddhism for the First Time   1

2   The Life of the Buddha   5

3   The Rise of Buddhism   9

4   Buddhism: Is it a Religion or a Philosophy?   13

5   Basic Beliefs and Teachings of Buddhism   17

6   Finding Your Inner Peace and Living the   23
Buddhist Way

A Final Word   29

INTRODUCTION

Interest in Buddhism usually begins with either the philosophy or psychology of Buddhism. Or maybe the esoteric nature of Buddhism, Buddhist meditation, or Buddhist wisdom. But the morality aspects of Buddhism are typically overlooked and frankly considered dull and boring. Keep in mind, however, that if you do not practice the virtues of Buddhism, your quest for the deeper aspects, such as enlightenment, will be similar to entering a tennis tournament without a racquet.

CHAPTER 1 – GETTING TO KNOW BUDDHISM FOR THE FIRST TIME

There are many religions practiced by people today such as Christianity, Islam, Buddhism, Judaism, Taoism, and Hinduism, among others. There are people, however, who do not associate themselves with any religion and they are commonly referred to as atheists. Most religions are focused on a Supreme Being or deity. In Buddhism however, the focus is not a god or deity but a way of life to find inner peace and avoid suffering brought about by worldly pleasures.

Buddhism is indeed a way of life. This religion has many facets that appeal to humanity making it the fourth largest religion in the world. Before you can incorporate Buddhism into your life, it is important to know what it is, who founded it, where it began, and the principles behind it. What is Buddhism really? Here are the basic things you need to know.

There are millions of people whose lives have changed because of Buddhism. As to its history, Buddhism is an old religion. It has roots from the 5th century BCE beginning from the life of Siddhartha Buddha. As history would tell, Buddhism had been the inspiration of successful civilizations as it was practiced by many prominent historical figures. Today, it is the fourth largest religion in the world and also one of the fastest growing religions. Many men and women from different ethnicities, political affiliations, and economic status practice Buddhism.

Unlike other religions, Buddhism is nontheistic. It is composed of traditions and beliefs which evolved from the life of the Buddha. It is nontheistic because followers of Buddhism do not worship a deity. Instead, they follow the ways of the Buddha— he who was born a man, lived as a man, and died as a man. What he left the world is his teachings and the choice to follow it depends on you.

Origins of Buddhism

Buddhism began in Asia and continually spread throughout the world. While Buddhism is a set of practices and beliefs, it has two major branches: Theravada and Mahayana. Theravada Buddhism or "The School of the Elders" is practiced in Southeast Asia while the Mahayana is practiced in East Asia. Buddhism is easy to understand and follow because of the structure of its principles. Numbers play a significant role in Buddhism which is evident in how it presents its precepts such as the four noble truths, the eight-fold path, the three jewels, and so on.

What is Buddhism then? In general, it is a moral philosophy founded upon the teachings of Buddha. Although designated as such, it is more than a philosophy because it is not merely search and love of wisdom but a set of precepts which is to be practiced until death. It is not like any other religion because it does not demand blind faith from people. Aside from the principles of pure living and thinking, there are no other dogmas, rites, or ceremonies practiced by Buddhists.

There were no written records of Buddha's teachings but it transcended through time because of his followers who preserved his teachings by committing it to memory. Buddha's disciples passed on his teachings orally from one generation to another.

After the Buddha's death, his teachings were compiled and called Tipitaka which contains all the essential teachings of Buddha. The Tipitaka is composed of three doctrines which are as follows: Vinaya Pitaka (The Basket of Discipline), Sutta Pitaka (The Basket of Discourses), and Abhidhamma Pitaka (The Basket of Ultimate Doctrine). Although the teachings of Buddha were preserved in books, it must be practiced.

As to the Buddhist texts, there is no single text subscribed to by Buddhist followers. There are several Buddhist scriptures which are written in different languages such as Pali, Tibetan, Chinese, and Mongolian, and some are even preserved in Sanskrit. This is logical because Buddha's teachings were passed on orally from one generation to another and there is no way that there exists a single text. It must be noted that the first monks of the sangha were given particular portions to memorize and pass on to younger monks. Although Buddha's teachings are not actually codified, the core of the path to enlightenment is well preserved.

M.E. Dahkid

CHAPTER 2 - GETTING TO KNOW BUDDHISM FOR THE FIRST TIME

Knowing what Buddhism is begins by drawing inspiration from the life of its founder, the Buddha. Siddhartha Gotama, the founder of Buddhism, was born 2500 years ago in Rummindei, a county near the border of India and Nepal. He was a fortunate man born into a royal family. His father, Suddhodana, was the Kshatriya king of a territory in the Nepalese Frontier. On the fifth day after Siddhartha's birth, the king called upon eight wise men to choose a name for the baby and to predict the child's future.

They chose Siddhartha. His name had a great significance in the path he chose to take because it means "one whose purpose has been achieved". The wise men also told the king that his son would eventually be an enlightened man searching for a path to enlightenment.

Siddhartha's mother, Queen Mahamaya, died on the seventh day after giving birth to him. Despite that, he grew to be a fine man and received the education fit for a prince. He became skilled in a lot of things such as arts and warfare. Like every father, Suddhodana wished for his son to marry a fine woman, raise a family, and eventually inherit his throne. However, the king's thoughts were bothered by the prediction of the wise men: that Siddhartha would leave his home and live the life of an ascetic.

As a prince, Siddhartha lived his life in luxury and comfort. His father, as much as possible, prevented him from feeling any sorrow. But the more King Suddhodana kept him away from sorrow, Siddhartha became more curious about the world. His eyes were opened to the cruel realities of the world when he saw an old man weakened with age asking for his help and the sight of a man who was merely skin and bones. While travelling along his father's territory, he saw kinsmen carrying a loved one for burial.

There are other instances when he came in contact with the outside world; the more he goes out of the castle, the more sorrow he feels. He was convinced that the world is an unhappy world—a world filled with sorrow and agony. He realized that there are three things which intoxicate man: youth, health, and life. These three, particularly the lack thereof, are the sources of sorrow according to the young Siddhartha.

By the time he was 29 years old, he left his life of comfort and luxury in his father's castle with a purpose in mind: to search for the true way to end suffering and be truly enlightened. He left the castle, his wife, his child, and renounced the crown. He took off his royal robes and wore a hermit's robe and headed his way to the forests and mountains of North-East India. He began his journey to enlightenment by studying different philosophies under the instruction of the wisest teachers of religion and philosophers of his time. He found out however that studying was not enough. Even self-mortification and extreme frugality were not enough to be enlightened.

After six years of self-mortification, he had not found what he was looking for but he did not lose his eyes on the goal of finding the way to enlightenment. By the time he was fully weakened, he realized that he could not have a successful search. Hence, he abandoned his self-torture and extreme fasting and returned to eating normal food.

By the time he was 35, he was able to find what he was looking for: the true enlightenment. In a secluded grove on the bank of the river Narenjara at Gaya which is now known as Buddhagaya, he sat cross-legged under a Bodhi tree. This tree is now known to be the "tree of wisdom" or "tree of enlightenment".

Using anapana pati or the mindfulness of in-and-out breathing, Siddhartha delved into his first meditative absorption known as the jhana. Gradually, he was able to enter different levels of jhanas until he finally cleansed his mind with impurities. By meditating, he was able to understood suffering, how it arises, how it can end, and the way to end suffering.

He also discovered the four noble truths whilst meditating under the Bodhi tree. Thus, on the full moon of May and at the age of 35, Siddhartha Gotama attained Supreme Enlightenment. He then became the Buddha, the Enlightened One. He spent his years teaching others the path to enlightenment until he reached the ripe age of eighty years. Although it has been thousands of years since Buddha passed away, his teachings about love, peace, wisdom, and charity remained.

What makes the life of Buddha different from the lives of those figures revered in other religions such as Jesus Christ and Muhammad? The answer is simple. Buddha did not become a deity whom his followers must praise and revere. His enlightenment did not come from a god or a supernatural being. He did not become a mythological figure. Instead, he is considered a model to attain true enlightenment.

When asked whether he became a god, an angel or a devil, the Buddha answered: "Just as, brahmin, a blue or red or white lotus born in water, grows in water and stands up above the water untouched by it, so too I, who was born in the world and grew up in the world, and I lived untouched by the world. Remember me as one who is enlightened." These words really show that the Buddha did not intend to pass himself off as a god. Instead, he must be considered a model that people should emulate.

Siddhartha Gotama was a man and continued to be a man although he became an extraordinary man. He is not a source of salvation for only you can end suffering but you can do it by following how the Buddha lived. Buddha teaches his followers that no one can grant deliverance to another. However, others may guide a person by teaching him the ways of the Buddha. As a teacher and as a model of how a person must live his life, the Buddha truly became an inspiration to many.

CHAPTER 3 - THE RISE OF BUDDHISM

After his enlightenment, the Buddha spent the rest of his life teaching the path he discovered mostly in the northern regions of India. His path, according to him, will lead others to be enlightened also regardless of race, creed, or sex. The only thing they need to do is to diligently follow his ways. Indeed, the history of Buddhism begins from the life of Siddhartha Gotama but after his death, his teachings remained and relayed up to the present time by his followers. This chapter deals with the rise of Buddhism after Buddha's death.

As stated earlier, the Buddha spent most of his time teaching the way to enlightenment. During the last 45 years of his life, he had hundreds of followers which are mostly ordained monks and nuns. Unlike today, Buddha's disciples did not live in monasteries. They were homelessand wandered in different places. With just three robes, a bowl for alms, a razor, a needle, and a water container, the monks lived their lives without worldly pleasures.

After Buddha's death, the first Buddhist council of monks convened headed by Mahakashyapa. He became the leader of the sangha whose first task is to compile the teachings of the Buddha which they memorized fervently. The monks recited and reviewed Buddha's teachings and for fifty years after the Buddha's death, the words were set in verse form which makes it easier to memorize.

Without its founder, there were several sects formed in the sangha which formed eighteen schools. There were no difference as to what they teach and each school coexists with the others. Students of the first Buddhist schools in fact studied and lived together. However, that did not prevent the formation of two distinct schools: Sthaviravada and Mahasanghika.

The first school is known as the "Way of the Elders". As the name implies, it is the conservative faction of Buddhism. The second school however proposed a more liberal approach to how monks should live. The rift between these two schools led to the second Buddhist council—a way to unify the sangha. That somehow was a failed attempt because the rifts remained and sectarian issues remained in the sangha. Because of the two schools of Buddhism that was formed, there were two Third Buddhist councils which dealt with issues of their time.

The Buddha laid down 227 rules for monks and 311 rules for nuns. Before his death, the Buddha said that some minor rules may be changed. This is where the two schools come in. Theravada Buddhism uses the Pali Canon. Mahayana Buddhism is in the Sanskrit language. Aside from the Pali Canon, Mahayana Buddhism has its own scriptures as well which includes the famous Lotus Sutra. At the onset, Buddhism spread slowly from India to other parts of Asia. However, it began to reach other territories when emperor Ashoka supported Buddhism and the subsequent expansion of the Mauryan Empire in Central Asia. Ashoka's descendants likewise supported Buddhism and that they constructed more memorials.

The evolution of the two Buddhist schools brought about the two schools of Buddhism known today: Theravada Buddhism and Mahayana Buddhism. Theravada Buddhism thrives in Sri Lanka, Thailand, Cambodia, Laos, and Myanmar while Mahayana Buddhism thrives in Japan, China, Taiwan, Nepal, Tibet, India, Korea, Vietnam, and Mongolia. The preservation of Buddha's teachings into written form and the growth of the Theravada and Mahayana schools made Buddhism flourish throughout Asia. Buddhism indeed has a rich history and it is continually practiced today. Buddhism as a familiar tradition in the East is continually becoming popular in the West.

M.E. Dahkid

CHAPTER 4- BUDDHISM: IS IT A RELIGION OR A PHILOSOPHY?

Whether or not it is a religion or a philosophy is the question which often comes out in every discussion pertaining to Buddhism. Buddhism is a moral philosophy but is considered the fourth largest religion in the world. What is it really? Is it a religion or a philosophy? Here are a few things you need to consider.

First, Buddhism is not a religion in the strictest sense of the word. Religion is defined as service and worship to God or a supernatural being. It also includes devotion to a religious faith. With these definitions, Buddhism really is not a religion because it is not a system of faith owing allegiance to a supreme being. Instead, it is a set of precepts leading to the path of deliverance.

Furthermore, it does not demand blind faith from people practicing Buddhism. It is in fact a guide to the ultimate happiness and avoidance of suffering. Unlike other religions which give assurance of salvation once you believe, Buddhism teaches that the Buddha cannot wash away others' impurities. Instead, the Buddha teaches that you are directly responsible for your purification. Although you seek refuge from the Buddha, the exercise of free will is still available and that you are in charge of gaining knowledge to be like the Buddha himself.

Looking into the actual practice of Buddhism today, one may argue that it is a religion because Buddhists worship images such as the Buddha or the Bo Tree. However, one must understand that followers of Buddha do not worship those images. Rather, it is a form of reverence to what these images actually represent such as Buddha's presence and enlightenment. You must take note that in Buddhism, you can avoid suffering and find inner peace not because of Buddha's intervention but because of your own actions.

There are no intercessory prayers in Buddhism and no matter how hard you pray to Buddha, you cannot be saved if you do not follow the teachings of Buddha and strive to be enlightened. As a Buddhist, you must win your freedom on your own.

As stated earlier, Buddhism is not strictly a religion because there is no god or deity to be feared and obeyed. There is neither heaven nor hell. There are neither revelations nor messages from deities. However, if religion would be defined as a teaching which guides life or if it provides ways to end suffering, then it may be considered religion.

Second, is it a philosophy? Although Buddhism is defined as a moral and non-aggressive philosophical system, it is more than a philosophy in the strictest sense of the world. Philosophy is simply defined as the search and love of wisdom. It is helpful to note that Buddhism is more than that. Although many books and articles state that Buddhism is a philosophy, it is more than that because it is not merely search and love of wisdom. Instead, it is a set of principles which guide human interactions until death.

Buddhism is different from other religions because it does not demand blind faith from those who follow the path of Buddha. Aside from the teachings of Buddha concerning pure living and thinking, there are no other dogmas, rites, or ceremonies that should be done. It all boils down to this: that Buddhism is a way of life. Whether some consider it as religion and others a philosophy, the teachings of Buddha remain influential. People are more inclined to follow a path that will lead to a happier and more compassionate life. So, regardless of its classification, many people choose to live the path Buddha had taken.

CHAPTER 5 – BASIC BELIEFS AND TEACHINGS OF BUDDHISM

Before knowing the basic beliefs and teachings of Buddhism, it is important to note that there are no hidden dogmas, secret beliefs, and hidden doctrines in Buddhism. This is anchored on the idea that the Buddha himself disapproves of secrecy. He once said, "Secrecy is the hallmark of false doctrines." What he knew of the ultimate path to enlightenment he also shared to all who listened to him without distinction. Also, it is important to note that Buddhism is not a forced way of life. It depends upon a person whether to follow Buddha or not.

As history provides, Buddhism was never forced upon anyone and neither was anyone compelled to be converted into Buddhism. Instead, what the Buddha left is a legacy of compassion, love, peace, and charity. If you want to know the path to enlightenment, it is necessary to know Buddhism's basic beliefs and teachings.

I.   The Way of Inquiry

As stated earlier, Buddhism does not require blind faith

from its followers. The Buddha himself warned people against it and encouraged them to know the way of truthful inquiry. In fact, blind adherence is foreign to Buddhism. The Buddha realizes that without blind faith, there can be no coercion, compulsion, persecution, or fanaticism. It appeals to the intellect more than emotion. Instead of requiring his followers to adhere only to what the Buddha says Buddhism is founded on a spirit of free inquiry and tolerance. What Buddha taught his followers is to have an open mind   and a sympathetic heart.

In one of his sermons, the Buddha pointed out that believing in something through hearsay, tradition, authority of ancient scriptures, word of a supernatural being, things learned from elders, and other sources may be dangerous.

What a person must do is to inquire using an open mind then he should reflect on his own life. If a way or view agrees to both experience and reason and it may lead to happiness, you should accept that view. Regardless of sex, age, or creed, Buddha's teachings are applicable if people would just inquire open-mindedly on what it offers. Although Buddhism began in Asia, it is not limited to the Asian way of life. Its application is not confined to where it originated because what it teaches is of universal application.

II.   The Four Noble Truths

Understanding and living the Buddhist way requires knowledge of the four noble truths: suffering, the cause of suffering, Nibbana (Nirvana), and the Middle Way or the eight-fold path. The four noble truths are the foundations of Buddhism so it is necessary to know them by heart if you are to live the Buddhist way. Whether Buddhism existed or not, these four truths will remain as they can be verified by human experience. It is rational and practical.

As already stated, the four noble truths are the center of Buddhist teachings. These are the four noble truths: (1) that all beings are afflicted with suffering; (2) that the cause of suffering is craving born out of the illusion of a soul; (3) that suffering will end when one achieves Nibbana; and (4) that enlightenment can be achieved through the Middle Way or the eight-fold path.

III.   The Eight-fold Path

To attain Nibbana (Nirvana), one must follow the eight-fold path or the Middle Way. The eight-fold path consists of the following:

(1) right understanding (samma-ditthi);
(2) right thoughts (samma-sankappa);
(3) right speech (sama-vaca);
(4) right actions (samma-kammanta);
(5) right livelihood (samma-ajiva);
(6) right effort (samma-vayama);
(7) right mindfulness (samma-sati); and
(8) right concentration (samma-samadhi).

The eight-fold path is also called the Middle Way because it is a balance between the two extremes of self-mortification and sensual indulgence. You must note that the Buddha himself found self-mortification insufficient to end suffering while sensual indulgence is harmful. Hence, it is good to be in between those two because the mind can only be clear and will have the ability to know the truth when one is not over-indulged and is in reasonable comfort. As you can see from the four paths, the Middle Way is really a cultivation of wisdom, virtue, and meditation.

Right understanding in Buddhism means the knowledge of the four noble truths. The Buddha said that to understand rightly, one must understand things as they really are and not what they appear to be. Right understanding will eventually lead to right thinking, hence the second component of the eight-fold path, right thoughts. Right thoughts serve a double purpose: to eliminate evil thoughts and to develop pure thoughts.

Also, it is a three-fold concept which includes renunciation of worldly pleasures (selflessness), loving kindness (benevolence), and compassion (harmlessness).

Right thoughts lead to right speech which is the abstinence from slandering, harsh words, and falsehood. Right speech leads to right actions which can be done by abstaining from sexual pleasures, stealing, and killing. The fifth component which is right livelihood means the ability to refrain from the five trades forbidden to lay disciples which are as follows: trading in arms, human beings, animals for slaughter, poisons, intoxicating drinks, and even drugs. Right livelihood also means that one should avoid hypocritical conduct and to achieve the requisites of monk-life the right way.

While right thought is three-fold, right effort is four-fold which consists of the following: discarding evil that has already arisen; preventing evil which may arise; developing good which may arise; and promoting good which has already arisen. Right mindfulness is being aware of the body, the mind, feelings, thoughts, and objects of the mind. Right effort and right mindfulness lead to the last component of the eight-fold path which is right concentration.

To understand it more clearly, the eight-fold path is divided into three: virtue, meditation, and wisdom. Virtue is composed of right speech, right action, and right livelihood. Followers must refrain from killing, stealing, sexual perversion, lying, and consuming intoxicating drinks or stupefying drugs.

Meditation includes right effort, right mindfulness, and right concentration. Meditation purifies the mind and allows the mind to have insights as to the meaning of life and how one must live. Wisdom includes right understanding and right thought. Through wisdom, one can know how to end suffering, transform his personality, and practice compassion.

IV. Kamma or Karma

Another important belief in Buddhism is the law of Kamma (Karma) which is translated as "action". Under this belief, all our actions have results. There are actions which may harm others, one's self, or both which is commonly referred to as bad kamma. Bad kamma is a result of greed, hatred, or delusion and they should not be done. There are also actions which are beneficial to others, to one's self, or both which is called good kamma. These actions are usually made out of compassion, generosity, and wisdom.

Unlike bad kamma, good kamma must be done often. What a person experiences is a result of kamma done in the past whether good or bad. The Buddha himself realized that there is no deity or supernatural being that controls the consequences of kamma. Instead, a person just reaps what he sows, good or bad. Hence, Buddhism encourages people to do good and avoid bad not because a greater being would reward them but because it is good kamma.

V. Rebirth

Understanding the law of Kamma makes it easier to understand rebirth. Kamma and rebirth explains why people are born into this world in unequal terms; some are wealthy and some are raised in poverty, some are healthy and some are not. Because it takes a long time before the fruits of Kamma can be realized, it should be understood in a framework of multiple lifetimes.

It must be noted however that when one is reborn unhealthy or in a state of poverty, it is not a punishment for bad Kamma done in previous lives but a lesson. It is also important to note that rebirth is not purely human. The Buddha pointed out that there are other realms aside from human. This is the reason why Buddhists never exploit animals for they feel that everything is connected because of rebirth.

VI. Nibbana (Nirvana)

Nibbana is the ultimate cessation of suffering in Buddhism. Many would call it enlightenment or awakening. People who are fully awakened and purified their minds of desire, ignorance, and aversion are deemed to have attained Nibbana. As seen from Pali texts, there are other people aside from Siddhartha Gotama who achieved the state of Nibbana. By following the eight-fold path and the teachings of the Buddha, one can end suffering and achieve Nibbana.

CHAPTER 6 – FINDING YOUR INNER PEACE AND LIVING THE BUDDHIST WAY

Enlightenment and the discovery of the precepts discussed in the previous chapter are not at all guided by divine providence. Instead, it is based on a person's initiative to seek enlightenment on his own by following the ways of the Buddha.

In fact, the enlightenment experienced by the Buddha himself can be repeated as it is not entirely unique; you can experience it yourself. The ways of the Buddha are open to anyone who seeks perfect wisdom and freedom from impurities brought about by worldly pleasures. Finding inner peace and living the Buddhist way is not a puzzle—whether you are all in or not at all. The reason is that Buddhism has no hidden agenda, no secret dogmas, and no secret doctrines. What the Buddha taught thousands of years ago remains the same until this day.

How can you become a Buddhist? There is a formal ceremony of taking the Three Refuges which is the

Buddha, the Dharma, and the Sangha. However, this ceremony alone does not determine whether or not you are a Buddhist for the true test is whether or not you incorporate Buddha's teachings into your life. Being a Buddhist does not require conversion; you are not obliged to renounce your religion or belief system if you do not want to. Being a Buddhist is a personal statement. Once you accept the teachings of Buddha into your life and follow the principles, you may be considered a Buddhist.

One essential thing in Buddhism is meditation. For you to find inner peace, it is important to meditate. You might ask what the relevance of meditation is in a successful Buddhist life. The aim of meditation is to clear the mind from things that may defile or disturb it. This is a precondition for the mind to gain insight and to understand the true nature of things. While meditating, a person becomes mindful and aware at the same time.

There are different ways to meditate as described in ancient Buddhist texts and it is up to the person to find the best method for him or her. As you already know, the way to freedom is personal and you have the power to find the most appropriate method for you. However, many people find the "mindfulness of breathing" very effective. After all, this is the same method the Buddha used to be enlightened.

Meditation is indeed important. However, it is also important to find the perfect spot where you can meditate. As many would suggest, you should look for a place which is quiet. A garden, patio, or any other spot you find peaceful may do well for a good meditation. To start, sit comfortably with your spine erect. Avoid leaning because it may cause drowsiness and you do not want that. Just relax and let your breath flow in a natural way. Do not force meditation. During meditation, your mind may wander off. You should not be afraid of that because it is natural especially when you are new to meditation. Twenty minutes of daily meditation may go a long way in starting your life the Buddhist way. By doing so, you can find inner peace.

Inner peace may seem absurd in this world full of hate, anger, and conflict. The root cause of these bad things is ignorance, anger, and desire. To have inner peace, one must overcome these three poisons. To find inner peace, one must overcome his selfish ambitions. Although it may seem an abstract idea, inner peace is a precondition to have peace inside the home, the workplace, and in the world. Having peace and incorporating it in all aspects of your life may lead to positive results such as good relationships. Inner peace is important in your journey to living a Buddhist life.

To help you out with the new path you wish to take, here are answers to some questions you may have regarding Buddhism.

Q: Will my prayers and offerings to Buddha bring me good karma?

A: Unfortunately, no. As already mentioned in the previous chapters, Buddhism is not a religion in the strictest sense of the word. There is no "god" that you can pray to who may bring good karma. Good karma is brought about by your actions. What you do in your daily life is what brings karma, not your prayers to Buddha. While there are rituals and practices in Buddhism such as offering flowers to Buddha, these are but additions to what the Buddha taught thousands of years ago in order to fill man's need for worship and expression. However, if you have good intentions in offering flowers and gold leaves to Buddha, it may bring good karma.

Q: How did the universe begin if there is no god?

A: It is important to note that the Buddha was more interested in finding an answer to how suffering can be avoided than to ponder upon the origins of the universe. In fact, the question as to where the world began is one that the Buddha refused to answer because he was aware that by doing so, he will open the path of enlightenment to controversy and debates. Furthermore, you must go back to the basic—that Buddhism is not a religion per se but a way of life to find inner peace and avoid suffering. According to the Buddha, it is not necessary to know the origin of the universe to find the true path to enlightenment. Instead, a person must find a way to end suffering.

Q: What is Nibbana? Is it heaven?

A: It is a mistake to compare Nibbana to heaven. First, Nibbana is not a realm which can be reached after death. Unlike the concept of heaven which can be reached after this life, Nibbana is to be attained while in this life. In its literal sense, Nibbana is the blowing out of causes which produce results in the cycle of life. Upon attainment of this realm, there will be no rebirth.

Q: Why is Buddhism very pessimistic in its view of life?

A: This is a question many people ask. Under the Buddhist tradition, people consider life as suffering. It may seem pessimistic at first but it is really not. In fact, it is an objective and realistic view of life, not sugar-coated and not giving false hopes. It is not even classified as pessimistic or optimistic; it's just is. When you meditate and when you ponder upon Buddha's teaching, you will realize that life in this world is centered on survival. Man's struggle to survive brings suffering and the only way to get out of that suffering is to realize that life indeed is suffering. Following the eight-fold path and clearing the mind will help you see the true nature of things, i.e. suffering brought about by worldly pleasures.

Q: Should I be a vegetarian and should I avoid alcohol even in moderate quantities?

A: It is a misconception that one has to be a 100% vegetarian to become a Buddhist. Buddha himself did not require his followers to abstain from eating meat because he realized that it would be difficult for people in different cultures to forego eating meat. The choice whether to eat meat or not is on you. However, you must know that whatever you do has karmic consequences. On alcohol however, even the smallest amount may affect your inhibition. It may affect the mind. If you are following the path of purification, it is best that you avoid it altogether. Since it is a way of life, you may have to give up some things you were accustomed to.

A FINAL WORD

Buddhism has now become a well-established aspect of the world - call it faith, religion, dharma or a way of life. Many see in Buddhism the potential to become a universal religion of futuristic world. I will conclude with a quote by Albert Einstein from 'The Buddha in the Eyes of Eminent Scholars' - "The religion of future will be a cosmic religion. It should transcend a personal God and avoid dogmas and theology.

Covering both the natural and the spiritual, it should be based on a religious sense arising from the experience of all things, natural and spiritual as a meaningful unity. Buddhism answers this description... If there is any religion that would cope with modern scientific needs, it would be Buddhism."

I want to take this time out to thank you for purchasing this book! The next step is to take action on the advice you've just read about.

Please Leave a Review

Finally, if you enjoyed this book, please take the time to share your thoughts and post a review on Amazon. It'd be greatly appreciated!

That review and feedback will help me improve the content in my books – and make each and every one more relevant and helpful to you.

Thank you again and good luck!

M.E. Dahkid

47240973R00024

Made in the USA
Lexington, KY
02 December 2015